Forever or a Week

Forever or a Week

Poems by

F.S. Blake

Cover design by Shay Culligan
Cover image *Boston Street Scene* by
Edward Mitchell Bannister (1828–1901),
courtesy of The Walters Art Museum on Unsplash
Author photo by F.S. Blake

ISBN: 979-8-90146-910-1
Library of Congress Control Number: 2026938827

Kelsay Books
502 South 1040 East, A-119
American Fork, Utah 84003
Kelsaybooks.com

To my children, who grew up with the good and bad of having a poet as a father

Acknowledgments

Grateful acknowledgment is extended to the editors of the following publications:

Cathexis Northwest Press: "Roadside Rattlesnake"
Coalitionworks: "A poem while you cook us dinner," "Laugh," "Birds"
Discretionary Love: "Fighting Every Day for You"
Duck Duck Mongoose: "one more log on the fire"
The Main Street Rag: "in the attic of bad memories," "Distillation"
Moonstone Arts Center: 29th Annual Poetry Ink: "One-Directional Sun"
Moonstone Arts Center: World Poetry Day Anthology: "Times in Between"
Oddball Magazine: "A poem while you cook us dinner"
Persimmon Review: "Muse"
Proud to Be: Writing by American Warriors (Laurel Review): "A heart like a cactus"
Quail Bell: "Flower Moon"
Rat's Ass Review: "The Magic of Goodbyes"
The RavensPerch: "Happier Songs"
San Pedro River Review: "if I took apart the pieces of a clock"
Welter at University of Baltimore: "Leave It in the Desert"
The Words Faire: "Joy," "spin faster, earth"

Contents

in the attic of bad memories 13
Leave It in the Desert 14
Distillation 15
What If Your Skin Were the Ocean? 16
Flower Moon 17
Without 18
Paradise 19
A heart like a cactus 20
In Order to Love the Plant 21
Saguaro 22
Birds 23
Hold On and Let Go 24
Roadside Rattlesnake 25
Laugh 26
Pact with Silence 27
Joy 28
Fresistance 29
Sideways Kisses 30
Closer 31
The Magic of Goodbyes 32
I Need Some Happier Songs 33
Reunion 34
it's okay to be selfish 35
Haint Blue 36
Comparison Game 37
game trails 38
Serendipity 39

Genius for Erotic Mischief 40
Forever or a Week 41
Wounded by the Lances of Nostalgia 42
Fighting Every Day for You 43
A Poem While You Cook Us Dinner 44
Muse 45
Affordance 46
Crystal Goblet 47
Times in Between 48
One-Directional Sun 50
And you should know your worth 51
Open your list of questions 52
spin faster, earth 53
I'll Tell the Stars 54
if I took apart the pieces of a clock 55
Winter 56
Yearning for a Lasting Springtime 57
now you must spin slower for me, earth 58
one more log on the fire 59

in the attic of bad memories

are tucked away
cobwebbed copies

of the lowlights of life
and old dented boxes

of lives lost and lingering lies
broken hearts and broken pieces

of plans that didn't pan out
and the deserts of happiness

suffering in drought
stored away and out of sight

the shinier sorrows of solemn strife
now in shadows craving light

left to gather the dust of decades
while life goes on in buzzing rooms below

Leave It in the Desert

Leave it in the desert.
Let the bone-dry winds that turn ancient
stones to sand howl across the face of your sorrows.

Feel the erosion of eons
wear the rough edges of what keeps you up at night,
down to the smooth sides of a cool pillow
beneath your life-weary head
as you look with hope towards constellations
devoid of city dilution.

Distillation

Let the growing sun swallow the colors
and, with its well-traveled rays,
purify your sadness that churns
in the chaparral of the soul.
Ruthless heat bakes from life
the moisture of too many tears.
For no man needs nothing,
and the vacuum of vistas sucks from us
life's complexities, leaves
in simple and silent harmony
those that can survive
on the desert
distilled.

What If Your Skin Were the Ocean?

The sea at rest before my eyes
Is smooth and beautiful
Serene stretches, soft seduction
Loving harbor embracing and soothing waves
Each inch lapping for exploration
Each tiny golden hair a perfect ripple
Your ink the medium of map makers
And the mark of maiden voyages
The inspiration of pilgrims, pirates, passions
If your skin were the ocean
I'd gently skim my hands across the surface
Set my sights on the horizon of your graceful curves
Yearning for the certainty
Of a tomorrow just like tonight.

Flower Moon

We sit on the shore, wear waves
like silk sheets, our fingers entwined.

The last Supermoon of the year
illuminates night shore secrets,

the hide-and-seek of evening crabs
and exposed bellies of starfish.

Lunar rays paint the waves
and shine on us as we stare in awe

at the closest we've ever been to the Moon
and each other.

Without

The coldest you will be is at night
When the lacking sinks its fingers in
Taking memories of the heat you had
The sun that's gone
The humid air you knew from other places
All absent now
In the icy silence of the desert
No lives chirping or machines whirring
No thoughts turning in the land
That yearns for what it once had
It's not the temperature that breaks you
It's that once, during the day, you had
The warmth you wanted.

Paradise

Mornings on the island of our sofa
Your fingers strum my forearm
As we sip coffee
Tree branches scrawl our names in cursive

Silence wraps us in a soft blanket

All the screens are asleep
We soak in the peace
Of only us

A heart like a cactus

Is conditioned by absence
Of kind water and vital words
And left to make due
In harsh landscapes
With what little it can draw
From deep desert roots
The residue of the necessary
Barely enough to survive
And with what's left over
Grows some fucking spikes.

In Order to Love the Plant

In order to love the plant
You have to love the flowers and the roots

Provide her with what gentle water she needs
To nourish, nurture, and conjure green shoots

To fully appreciate the beauty of the flower
You must understand the mystic source of her power

Elegance experienced by all those around
Has its beginnings in the dark and fertile ground

Grand Architect's flawless petal
The blossom of a woman who should never settle.

Saguaro

Chaparral, saguaro, sweet foreign chirps
Of unnamed birds
Cool night sky, constellation curtain drawn,
Sun still warming up—
And at rest before me
The great stage of the Southwest,
Set design
For adventure only the desert can provide.

Birds

In a life where I have loved you before
Perhaps we were both birds
Loving each other again to our core
Snuggling in our nest without needing words

Two creatures so perfectly aligned
Because we loved in a past life
In all incarnations we always find
Our love that always conquers strife

Each time it is my heart's true pleasure
To look and look and look till I find
The soul that will always be my greatest treasure
So to her I myself may once more bind

As birds our happiness would easily soar
On to our next life where I will love you even more.

Hold On and Let Go

Hold on, and let go
And move so fast
The sorrows you know
Shrivel in the sand.

Speed up and slow down
And tell everyone who will hear,
Come gather 'round
Burn the gods with our deepest fears.

Don't run away from life
For you are still its master:
Life is a copperhead wound around himself.
Ride away, it's faster.

Roadside Rattlesnake

Thick triangular head
Awake and aware and telling you
To dare take one more step—
It had been self-isolating in the bush, you see
Not that different from you and me
Quick to anger and quick to strike
Not a drop of patience for the meaningless
Cul-de-sac conversation of suburban exile
Or the mundane tasks of the mediocre world
People with dimly-lit eyes who populate
The scenery with the frequency of the saguaro
And the folks who ask, but never understand
What it means to feel this way:
Temper at a constant near-boil
Volcano on a perpetual edge of eruption
The infinite mousetrap spring
I'm tired of how angry I've become
And I'm having a hard time holding back the venom
At any second I could give into my rage and let fly with fangs—
At least the snake can warn them.

Laugh

When you called my laugh a siren
was it because
I can slap the switch while chasing happiness through the streets
of a new city
or because my
volume and pitch rise and fall in crescendos and crash waves
of wedding joy incarnate
or
because hidden behind the sine and sounds of satisfaction are
the eternal undertones of wailing, warning

Pact with Silence

I have an honorable pact
With silence
A handshake with stillness
Alone
In the silence of solace
And comforted
By the absence of others
Turning down the volume knob
Of internal dialog and discord
Blocking out

The noise of the known and influence of outsiders
Agreeing to trade the benefits of busy worlds
For the peace found only
Within

Joy

Alone in the safety of new love
And together in the harmony of constant alignment
We fused our hearts to the deeper parts
Of the cosmic sources of feelings

Words, unable to capture the meanings
Or form the unfathomable edges of feelings,
Dissolve their pieces first into letters and lines
Then to blank pages unknown authors prescribed

Outside of fate, languages falter and fail to convey
Sentences struggle and dictionaries sit blank
Heavy with dust, save for the one clear word
She's drawn on my heart.

Fresistance

Resist and rationalize
Get distracted and take your eyes from all you should consider
Your prize

Stay busy and don't start
No progress towards what brings joy to your weary heart

Surrender the struggle for your authentic roots
Stay placid, let dust gather on your adventure boots

Easier for us to ignore our inner light—
We've fought our wars. We're not eager for another fight.

Sideways Kisses

Our lips can't meet head on.
In their way: obstacles, roadblocks,
The accumulation of life—
To-do lists stick to our skin.
Our ears hold whispers of past lovers.

Passions kept in cages,
We dance along edges,
Peck our way towards
What our hearts know.

Hints and preludes to our romantic epic unleashed,

Our foreheads touch,
Your breath on my cheek—
At long last our lips meet.

Closer

Foreheads touching bodies entwined
The blurry world swirls
outside these walls creating the stage for our romance
to roam Forces that draw us together
freeze clocks turn the intricate keys
for passion to unlock magical incantations
of laughter's sweet and soothing songs
Our hearts attract ancient spells
producing the exquisite proximity of our skin and our souls
so we beg the question
Could we get any closer?

The Magic of Goodbyes

Our goodbyes keep getting harder
Each one building upon the last
Tears stacked on soaked shoulders
And new words conjured daily
For sadness, longing, and love.

Strange dictionaries
Printed at each parting to serve as brutal
Reference for hearts rendered molten
And bodies ripped from each other as we mourn
The magician's bird stuffed back in his hat.

I Need Some Happier Songs

Whose upbeat tones and joyful cries
Distract me from your absence

They should summon new loves
Or soothe with the contentment of reunion

Let hearts fold into each other
Whether with bodies at rest or in motion

Calm oceans and clear whole skies
Leave your smiles in my ears

Despite the winding miles
Or the adventures of new partners

I need songs
About holding hands

Played by marching bands
Trumpets growing stronger

All to help me forget
That once you were here

But no longer.

Reunion

From my anguish she delivers
With the act of one noble kiss
By the soft bank of swollen rivers
Our reunion, pure bliss

Time apart has been so hard
Charged hearts, constant moving
Distant love has left us scarred
Healed now by kisses' soothing

Our embrace delivers us content
From an absence far too long
And turns longing's bitter lament

Into joy's ecstatic song

For we're starved of peace until the time when
Our linked souls are reunited again

it's okay to be selfish

and save for yourself
the moments and molecules

of happiness too often withheld
filter and catalog them within lives

create a hazy fog that could be shared
but serves as a secret source

of singular contentment

fuel for an individual joy

Haint Blue

Trick our ghosts
With a lighter shade of blue
Send them sailing
Past their haunting destinations
Through the traps of our colors
Their intention unknown
We vault them into false skies on porches
And protect us with moats of indigo
So that the sorrows that chase us
Can move on down the block
To neighbors not protected
By the lighter shade
Of our blue
Haint

Comparison Game

Open your books
and with learned hands flip through forlorn pages
archived memories from the greatest days
Set your stage for the reincarnation
of ephemeral smiles captured on forgotten films
Tear open the scars that cover your nostalgia and discover
new joys you couldn't feel when the wounds were oozing, fresh
Your beauty and joys, unknowable then,
seize their chances to sing and dance
celebrations of deferred happiness
Memories better than on the days of their creation
lie stuffed in volumes: instruction manuals
for the comparison game

game trails

meander through the mind
the lazy thoughts you permit
the kind that are part of the landscape by now
timeworn and trodden trails of ifs and thens
left alone, your thoughts will stay the course
unless, through force
the hunter blocks the source
and frees his game
to roam the mind's endless landscape

Serendipity

The cosmos conspiring for the benefit of our hearts
The universe unveiling its grace to us in the form of found
    hours
together
so that I could gaze upon your loveliness longer
and get lost in the luxury of your timeless beauty
The pressing of all possibilities
into the once clear eventuality
where it is just you and me
We soak in blissful conversations
gifted to us by benevolent gods
who smile at two mortals who've found riches
usually reserved for the heavens
The lucky leaps taken with wild abandon and the joys
of our smiles when we always stick the landing
The sweetness of plump moments we wouldn't have
were it not for this serendipity—
The world winds to a stop
so that we can wring from clocks the minutes and measures
that serve as the infinite source of our happiness

Genius for Erotic Mischief

When we two, our bodies meet
And passion's clasp unhinge
We relent to urges sweet
And begin our carnal binge

It starts with several playful glances
Knowing exactly what we seek
Stolen hours and stolen chances
Starting out for our peak

Wandering hands and volleys of kisses
Our desires reach for more
The culmination of secret wishes
Our fantasies open to explore

The pinnacle of creative lust
Built on foundations of loving trust

Forever or a Week

Has it been forever or a week
Since first our lonely hearts were fused
Now soaking in the views from passion's peak
The journey of our souls no longer confused

For although I've known you but a short time
It's obvious this love is meant to be
Starting today we declare you mine
Destined to set each other's happiness free

It's proof that love can happen fast
And in an instant your life can spin
Now focused on our future instead of our past
Eager for our new life to begin

People won't believe me when I say
I'll love you forever starting today

Wounded by the Lances of Nostalgia

Wounded by the lances of nostalgia
Knight errant clutching his chest
Struck by pangs of his past
Gone are days considered his best
His current quest his last

Stabbed by opportunities lost
Longing for memories by his side
Unable to cover the cost
The joys of his past now denied

Our hero at the end of his rope
Killed by what he misses
Last moments devoid of hope
Brought from love and kisses

Sorrow for the past the source
Of his death hastened by remorse.

Fighting Every Day for You

I fight every day for you
to show you
the infinite and inestimable value of your worth
To prove to you
the depths of my love and to reveal the eternal spring
from which it flows
To demonstrate its purity, unrivaled in history, unblemished
and polished to a flawless shine
To offer what little I can to help sway
your heart towards mine and your gaze on my longing eyes
To protect you
from the evils I've seen in the world,
not for any reason other than an innate desire to wrap you up
and make everything right for you
To impress you
through acts large and small and necessary or not
but all designed to show you I'm capable and worthy
of your affection
I fight every day for you
to believe

A Poem While You Cook Us Dinner

I can see you
Pouring love into every ingredient
And joy for our future in every recipe
Care in your moves and passion in each dish you stir
The selflessness of the chef
The focused intensity of the lover
The elation of the artist
And the care of a true partner
Every bit more delicious than the last
Flavored by a genuine and eternal love

Muse

When old muses hide their grace
And I'm searching for a line
All I do is see your face
And the words start flowing just fine

Your eyes and lips they do inspire
Words for a thousand books
And I the poet do acquire
Courage and strength from your looks

Joyfully recalling the days of our past
Your lyrics begin their start
To capture in ink at long last
Secret passageways of my heart

For when our weary hearts did fuse
You immediately became my forever muse.

Affordance

The obvious operation
Of heartbeats' rhythms
Restored to birdsong
The guide of intuition
The knowing and known touch
And the seamless operation
Of our two bodies
When they meet in passion's sweet embrace.

Crystal Goblet

Drink deeply from the Crystal Goblet
Rest your sanguine lips on its edge

And prepare to receive an elixir brewed to satisfy

Your need, to quench your thirsty soul

With liquid incarnations of safety, love, and kindness
Infused with timeless chanted incantations

Sung by healers, danced around ancient fires
With shouts of passion and primal knowledge

Bodies fused in sex
Taste of golden sun rays penetrating a lover's forest

Its warmth on your tongue
Is the gentle heat of lips that meet in ecstasy

And delicious
As the extra hours of late-night confessions

Drink deeply from the Crystal Goblet
And let it serve to satisfy the driest parts of neglect

And heal the inner workings of the most beautiful
The Gods have ever known.

Times in Between

Dance with me in the intermission
And let's play in the preludes
Our main events are sold out shows
But secretly I have an admission

I long for the time in between

We can motivate, and moderate, and arrive on time
And we can operate, and execute, and do things just fine

But I live for the moments in between

We can hustle, and haggle, and hurry to catch flights
Or work, or study, or discuss civil rights

But for me what matters is the time in between

You could wear a gown and I a tuxedo
Or we could lock ourselves away and give in to our libido

Sometimes, what's better is the time in between

Our parties and our dinners
And all our chances to show the world we are fucking winners

Are powered by the time in between

Where countless hours dissolve
And hearts are buttressed with resolve
Where lists and agendas disappear
And two lonely hearts draw near

Subjects waiting while a King enjoys his Queen
Not in public
But in the times in between

One-Directional Sun

Here, the sun has rays that shine in one direction
Emanating wild nuclear birth spasms
And hot molten elemental precision
From a secret core towards their mortal destination
Facing only one way and leaving great wide swaths
Of the universe cold, untouched.

This sun that shines in only one direction
Drips its rays with favoritism on faces
That have only known sunrises
And islands that can't sell sunset postcards.

The rays go the only way they know
And leave in absolute Kelvin isolation
Many would-be baskers
So that we can feel the heat of celestial obsession.

And you should know your worth

is the ultimate expression of what the ancient gods imagined
when they created the words for beauty

The purity of your heart projected for the world through a smile
that draws me close and renders a cactus spikeless

Your flawless form and the curves that fuel obsession
and loose the shackles of erotic exploration

Your passion, the dormant volcano, now roaring to life
as the hard rocks of hard lives
are rendered molten by the continents of our worlds colliding

You should know your worth and toss into the deserts
the desolation

where those that don't know
know it also.

Open your list of questions

and ask me
the queries and quandaries that now serve
as thick woven ropes pulling us together
Let the answers dance as angels
encouraging new lovers across the tightrope
towards their first embrace
And let the deeper knowledge of each other
pull the fine threads of veils
leaving bare our faces to look upon each other
and know our answers without saying a word.

spin faster, earth

and twist upon your axis
with anxious hope after longing
speed the journey round yourself
that marks the torturous days
of absence and polar separation
accelerate your pace in lock step
with your understanding
of the pain I feel
created by the distance
of days
spin faster earth
and pull forward that reunion
that brings wildflowers to my heart
and opens fields in my mind

I'll Tell the Stars

When stars shine down on me at night
after the storm clouds and raindrops part,
and stars cast their shiny brilliance across the blank
slate of a cool new night—I'll tell them
about you.

They'll hear me whisper your name in awe
and listen to my breathless gratitude for you
filling my life—I'll tell the stars all about you.

When I look up to them after a long day
and a short sunset, they'll hear me shout
the joy you've brought me and will catch
the echoes of my love that shines more brightly
than they could ever dream—I'll tell the stars
it's always been: you.

if I took apart the pieces of a clock

and placed in piles
all the gears and hands
springs and bands,
could I unlock their secrets—
dissolving multitudes of machinations
that force on their march
millions of moments—
could I sort through each second
heaping aside the hours
and wandering through their mysteries—
if I could disassemble the whole puzzle,
I would do all these things
just to find our one moment together
so I could stretch it into an infinity—

Winter

In winter, summer heat is traded
For icy chills and skies too faded
Splashes in lakes and pools quickly swapped
For hot chocolate and cuddles as temperatures drop
Like weather, our connection evolves through all seasons
Annual revelations of the countless reasons
That finding each other was cosmic fate
You, my *every* season eternal soulmate

Yearning for a Lasting Springtime

I am yearning for a springtime that never stops

One without winters' icy cliffs
Or summers' steamy grips

A season of awakened birds in mild mornings

And lotus flowers sprung forth from the rivers of Macondo

A season stretched through a temperate infinity

Bereft of the fears of fall
And safe in the eternal newness of constant birth

I am yearning for forever springtime

Green shoots
And satiated roots

A time of healing rains
Warmer evenings
And small-town lovers preparing for marriage

A stretch soaked with sunshine

I won't miss the winter
No, I will bask in the radiant rays of unwritten opportunity

now you must spin slower for me, earth

measure your steps, your meter, your cadence.
please, take your sweet time
to amble about your apogee
in no particular hurry.
as for me,
I've found what I have been searching for,
as fleeting as it may be.
I ask you to stretch this moment into millennia—
to bask in this eternal now.

one more log on the fire

resets our timer
means the moment's not up
conversations extended
reload on crackle
and the slimmer cord
adds minutes to the clock
keeps tomorrows at bay

About the Author

F.S. Blake is a Bronze Star decorated U.S. Army Veteran and Pushcart Prize-nominated poet. His poetry career began during his sister's wedding. Blake is also a published photographer, traveler, advanced SCUBA diver, philanthropist, entrepreneur, and proud father.

He has poems published or forthcoming in *The Military Review, Welter at University of Baltimore, San Pedro River Review, Cathexis Northwest Press, Persimmon Review,* and *The Main Street Rag,* among others. His chapbooks, *Terminal Leave, Above the Gold Fields,* and *The Few Drops Known,* are available from Finishing Line Press.

www.ingramcontent.com/pod-product-compliance
Lightning Source LLC
LaVergne TN
LVHW090537110826
845146LV00003B/1144

* 9 7 9 8 9 0 1 4 6 9 1 0 1 *